eBay Selling

7 Steps to Starting a Successful eBay Business from $0 and Make Money on eBay – Be an eBay Success with your own eBay Store (eBay Tips Book 1)

by Ashton Pereira

Ashton Jude
TheBigVenture.com

Table of Contents

Who is this book for?

Do you want to start making money online?

Are you interested in making money on eBay?

Has the idea of having a passive income from eBay interested you?

Well then this book is for you!

Included in this book is a fully detailed 7-step guide that will take you from $0 to potentially earning a passive income online through eBay!

Let me explain how...

What will this book teach you?

This book contains every step of the process that you need to be aware of if you want to start your own successful eBay business.

I have included everything you need to know from creating your eBay and PayPal accounts, to automating your entire eBay selling processes so that you can take your business all the way to a six-figure income.

But what about finding profitable products?

Yes, I have that too!

I know how important finding profitable products is to an eBay business, it's the most important factor. So…

I've included an entire chapter telling YOU exactly how I find profitable products and how you can too!

Step 1 - It Starts with You...

To be successful on eBay you have to possess a particular type of mindset that is original and different to everyone else. You have to be persistent and able to learn new things quickly, adapting to the market or to your customers as demand changes.

Put simply though, there are five traits that by possessing give you an increased advantage over many others attempting to start their own eBay businesses.

1) You have to be a quick learner

It doesn't matter if you're coming into starting an eBay business as a complete beginner who doesn't have an account on eBay, or someone who buys and sells a few items every month, starting and growing a successful business online will involve you to learn many new things.

I'm going to be teaching you a lot in this book and getting you started on the right track, showing you the exact path that you can take to go from $0 to potentially hundreds of thousands a year in revenue from your very own eBay business!

That being said, if you truly possess the mindset to succeed at your own eBay business, you will also have the desire to find out more, learn more, and hopefully earn more in the long run. This is something that won't change, and if you feel that this describes you, then you've definitely got the potential!

As you can see, the learning never stops, so you need to be able to learn quickly and apply what you learn to your business.

2) Accept that you don't know

This may not apply to everyone, but if you're someone who has a slightly larger than average ego, you need to accept that you don't know. You have to look for help, take it when it's offered to you, and learn.

As simple as this may sound, a lot of people can get caught up in believing that they know everything, especially after the first few months running a profitable eBay store. The truth is that you *never* know everything, and you should *always* be learning.

The sooner you realize this, the more you will improve.

3) Awareness that your business comes first

When you begin your pursuit towards a successful eBay business, you may not see it as a business, rather just a little side hobby. This limiting belief will end up being the most destructive thing to your business.

An eBay business is no difference to any other business you may have, in that you're main objective should be to make profit while providing value to your customers.

You need to source products at a lower cost than you can sell them for (after including other selling fees into the equation). Your eBay business it not a hobby, you shouldn't be giving away inventory for free to your friends, and you should definitely not be dipping into your inventory for your own personal use.

If you treat it like a hobby, it will never be anything else!

4) Networking skills

Just like if you had a brick and mortar business, networking and building relationships with both your customers and also your suppliers is a very important aspect of your business.

Just because your store is online and you're sitting behind a computer screen, you should never fall into the trap of believing that your business deals with anonymous transactions.

Yes, you may not know what your customer or suppliers look like, but there are real people behind those computer screens on the other end of the transaction, and if you appeal to them personally, this will be the biggest advantage you could have over your competition.

Just like customers may feel loyal toward a particular supermarket for their groceries, they can also feel loyal toward an online store for a certain product (hopefully YOUR product!).

5) Desire!

Finally, what I would consider to be the most important trait you need to have to make it big in this business – desire!

You have to want to succeed with your eBay business, no matter the time involved, the costs involved, and the sacrifices you have to make.

If you really want to succeed with this and make it a business, rather than a small part time hobby, you can do it.

Never forget that you cannot fail unless you stop trying!

So above are the most important traits I feel are desirable to have if pursuing an eBay business. "What if I'm not good at networking?" you may ask?

Well the truth is this. If you could only have one of the above traits, it would have to be number five or I wouldn't recommend attempting to start your own eBay business. However, keeping in mind that you're reading this, I think you're definitely ready to begin your own eBay business, and as long as desire is there, since you're now aware of the other traits, they will come in time!

Step 2 – eBay & PayPal Accounts

Before we get into the exciting bits about how we're going to make lots of money from our eBay business, we have to get the basics under control.

Firstly, we need an eBay account set up as a selling account. If you already have an eBay account keep reading because I have some important advice that can help you nevertheless.

If you don't have an eBay account, make sure you go to the right eBay website. You want to add the right prefix after the domain name "eBay". Here are the most common ones: USA (.com), Australia (.com.au), UK (.co.uk), Canada (.ca). Once you're on the right site, simply follow the steps to create an account, it's quite simple and self-explanatory.

When choosing your eBay account name, keep in mind that it's going to the name visible to your customers when you start up your eBay business, so choose wisely. That being said, after 30 days you can change your eBay username. So, if you already have an eBay account, you can continue to use it as your business account and just change the username.

PayPal

Once you have your eBay account set up, go over to PayPal (http://www.paypal.com) and create an account if you don't already have one. Once you go to the main PayPal site it will redirect you to your country's PayPal site so that the main currency is the currency you will do business in.

Making a PayPal account is also straightforward, and the reason we do it is because it's the main payment method that is used by eBay users around the world. Additionally, it gives buyers protection, in that they can dispute any issues that arise when purchasing products online. As a seller, you should be aware of this because it means you should ensure you deliver great customer service and stick to your policies specified in your listings (more about this later).

Once we begin selling items on eBay, we will be prompted to enter our PayPal address into eBay because they require a payment method linked to our eBay account for monthly fees to be deducted. If you don't already know, eBay charges fees to sell items, they charge approximately 10% of the selling price (it varies depending on location – so I suggest a quick Google search of "eBay selling fees in xxx" – with xxx being the country you're located in).

eBay fees aren't a worry for us though, because we're going to maximize our revenues to allow enough profit even after eBay fees.

Another thing to also note is that PayPal charges fees too, albeit smaller than eBay fees, but still there. They are usually no more than 3%, but as suggested above, a Google search here will suffice in finding out what the exact fee is.

eBay Powerseller

Being a Powerseller on eBay is simply a status that represents the fact you have been selling for at least a few months, and have achieved a minimum standard of feedback and ratings from all your sales.

You can find out more about how to become a Powerseller, and the benefits of being a Powerseller right here:

http://pages.ebay.com/help/sell/sell-powersellers.html

All you really need to know about being a Powerseller is that it's a great benefit to have when you have your own eBay store, because it gives you an extra boost of reputation to customers, however it's not needed. You can run a massively successful eBay business without being a Powerseller, and if it happens, it happens!

Just keep in mind that being a Powerseller is something that happens automatically based on your results as a seller. You can't apply, it's just a status given to you!

eBay Store

An eBay store is something that you have complete control over (not like being a Powerseller). Having an eBay store is not a status, rather it's a way you can demonstrate and show to your customers that you have a specialized store and you're a business, rather than just being an average Joe selling extra bits and pieces from around the house.

There are many benefits from having an eBay store, and I highly recommend it (depending on your circumstances, maybe no at the beginning of your selling career, but definitely down the track when revenues and your product ranges begin to pick up).

Not only do you have access to many marketing features when you have an eBay store, but you can also create discounts, hold cross promotions, promote flyers about certain products of yours, and you can even embed your eBay store into your own website if you wish to sell from a website too. Additionally, you can do many customizations and modifications to both your eBay selling page and your About page when you have an eBay store.

The biggest benefit though, is lower listing fees. As mentioned before, fees are different depending on what country you're in, so check that. But as a general statement it's true that listing fees are cheaper when you have an eBay store because they are there for sellers who are working with many, many products.

There are fees to have an eBay store, and this is what you need to account for. It's profitable to have an eBay store in the long run if you are selling many items, and this is why I advise most likely against an eBay store when beginning your selling career and only selling 1-5 product lines.

Step 3 – Turning $0 into $500+

Now that your account is all set up and the necessities are in order, we can get to the good stuff!

This is where I get to teach you exactly how I started off selling on eBay with absolutely $0 in my pocket, and turned it into a successful business that earned me upwards of $20,000 **profit** in my first year, and $55,000 **profit** in my second year!

I also recommend that if you haven't already downloaded your FREE Action Plan that goes with this eBook, to download it because it will make implementing all my strategies much easier.

http://www.thebigventure.com/ebay-business-action-plan/

Okay, so this entire step (or chapter) has two main objectives:

1) To give you at least $500 worth of capital to be able to use in your business and get things started.

2) To allow you to learn how eBay works, receive some selling feedback, test out different features, and get some experience packing and shipping items.

If you already have money to invest in your business, I still advise you to at least give this step a brief skim because I will be including several great tips on how to sell items for more money than you could normally get them for!

Let's get started...

The way you're going to raise capital for your business is by searching through your house for any items you don't need anymore, but contain value that still allows you to sell it online.

I'm sure you have heard about people doing it before, turning junk into cash. It's totally possible, and when I was only 16 years old I converted some of my old gaming consoles and trading cards into $500 cash (after fees and shipping costs)!

The best way to approach this is to go through your own belongings room-by-room. Create a pile of things in each room of the stuff you no longer need but believe has value. Also, keep a pen and paper with you and create a list of these things, so you can sit down at your computer later and check what prices the items might go for, as well as some additional product research (all of which I will discuss in detail later). So, what exactly are you looking for?

Kitchen

- Cookware, especially any antiques or old ones you have collected over time. Many people acquire porcelain cookware over the years. You may even have some new items in boxes that you got as gifts and never really needed or used.

- Appliances that you no longer need in the kitchen, or were gifted and never used.

15

- Junk on the fridge, usually tourist magnets or collector magnets from certain cities in the world can go for a lot of money on eBay. People collect magnets and would love to pay top dollar for your fridge junk!

Living Room

- Any decorative items, paintings, lamps, or furnishings that you never really liked or were planning on getting rid of can serve perfectly as that initial capital for your business!

- If you have any old VHS tapes, recorders, CDs, DVDs, books, etc., which you no longer use anymore, yet again there are plenty of people surfing eBay every night looking for old items like these that they can add to their personal collections.

- Instead of throwing out any furniture, list it on eBay first. Remember that you don't have to offer shipping all the time, you can offer "pick-up" which means the buyer will come to your home or office and pick up the furniture.

Basement/Storage Room

The basement/storage room is probably going to be the most profitable room for you, especially if this is where you store all your stuff!

- Let's begin with DVDs, VHS tapes, recorders, satellite receivers, and other similar devices. A lot of these can be obsolete but don't underestimate them based on this, a lot of people on eBay collect such items.

- If you have any cameras, video recorders, mp3 players, speakers, televisions, etc., they are also great to sell because these usually go for even more.

- This is what I sold to make most of my initial capital; video game consoles and old computers or laptops go for great amounts on eBay and if you sell maybe two or three of these you could end up surpassing $500 right here. Keep in mind a lot of older video game consoles actually sell for surprising amounts because they have retained vintage value.

- You may also have other antiques, board games, collector items and things like these.

- Finally, don't forget books! Despite living in a very technological world where most books are available online (quite like the one you're reading now), you can still sell a book online for anywhere from $1 to $10, depending on the title. I personally had 72 old books that I didn't want and none had any decent value. I ended up selling 61 of them for a total profit of $76 profit after all fees, and then donated the remaining 11 books to a local thrift shop. The point here is that even if they go for $1 or $2 individually, when you start bulking about these piles of items together, you will realize you're selling a large amount of goods so every dollar counts!

Bedroom

- The first place to go in your bedroom is straight to your closet. Take a look at your clothes and see if you can identify any clothes you haven't worn in a long time or that don't fit you anymore. If you have kids, take a look at all the clothes that they have grown out of and put them into the "sell" pile. Once you create a pile of these items, because they are clothes I suggest just looking through once more and ask yourself if you would buy this (in terms of its quality). Remembering you are trying to build up a lot of positive feedback, you only want to be selling good quality items. The bargain items here are the ones you bought or were gifted and never wore at all, or only wore once or twice.

- The next place is shoes! Despite the initial assumption by many that no one would ever buy second hand shoes, especially when it comes to shoes that have been worn just a handful of times, you can actually be very far from the truth! Again, quality matters here and simply ask yourself if you think it's in good enough condition to sell.

- This one is especially profitable if you have kids, but go through their room and grab all the toys that you know they don't play with anymore. Kids commonly grow out of toys within months, sometimes weeks, and you can easily be selling these back on eBay to make money!

- Finally, go through any old jewelry that you may have. Once again rule number one applies; simply look for things you haven't worn in a long time and don't feel you need, and sell it on eBay.

Garage

- If you have any old car parts, or bicycles, motorbikes, or even old cars that you have been meaning to sell or don't really want, now is your chance! Put it up on eBay and tick the box to allow "Pick Up" rather than shipping, meaning that the buyer will come by your place and pick the item up and it's their responsibility. A great positive from this is that if you get paid in cash, you don't have to worry about PayPal fees!

- There's a chance you may have some old sporting equipment lying around, things like fishing rods, golf clubs, or even gym equipment. If you don't use these anymore they are also great things to use for your initial business capital.

At this point I'm sure you've gotten the point and understand that there are many, many options and ways to raise capital from absolutely nothing.

The above advice was merely suggestive, and you can even contact friends and family and grab some bargains off them that they no longer want anymore. Maybe help them sell their old items and they could give you a few bucks for helping them out!

Remember that if you're not sure if something has any value, just jump on eBay and search it. Check if anyone else is selling the same thing and how much he or she is selling it for!

Also, just to answer the most common question people ask me at this point – it's completely fine to sell second hand items on eBay. When you actually begin doing some product research on eBay you will see that the vast majority of people selling items on eBay are actually selling pre-owned items.

When creating your listing for your items, be sure to include any faults with the item, or even if there are any non-removable stains or scratches.

Also include whether the item is in good condition, excellent condition or near-new condition.

As I said, simply do some product research and you will see how people structure their listings and describe issues with second hand items if there are any.

Now let's take a look at the other benefits of doing this, other than to raise initial capital.

The Best Way to Learn

One of the biggest benefits to selling stuff from around your house to begin your journey to running a succcssful eBay business is that it gives you a chance to learn how eBay works.

It gives you the chance to play around with the many listing features, and experience packing and shipping fees firsthand so you can estimate them more accurately in the future.

Get That Feedback

The more positive feedback you have, the more reputable you seem as an eBay seller to your customers.

To eBay, however, they see a difference between buying and selling feedback, rightly so. Hence, positive feedback from selling items will give you even more points with eBay, since it shows that you're a solid eBay seller.

So now that you know why you're doing it, how can you go about selling these initial items for the most money?

Here are 4 eBay tips that will drastically increase the sale price of your items

1) Listing your item as an auction

Whether you're already an active eBay user or not, when you start listing items up on eBay you will notice that there are many options and features you can apply to your listing. One of the most important of these options is whether you choose to list your item as a "Buy It Now" or an "Auction".

An "Buy It Now" listing means that you set the price you want to sell your item for, and it's up to the buyer to decide whether or not they want it for that price. This is pretty much like going into a store and buying an item; the buyer has no ability to change the price, what's stated is the price.

There is an option to also include a "Best Offer" option on a "Buy It Now" listing, meaning that the buyer can actually send in an offer to you, which is below the listed price, and you have the choice whether or not to accept it. This is the same as a one-offer negotiation.

The other option, which is what I suggest you do, is to list the item as an auction. The reason is because you can allow multiple buyers to take part of your selling process and help determine the price based on the market value, and using the tips I list below, you can maximize the sale price of your item even when using an auction.

It's wise to check the value of the item you're selling on eBay (just search it before you list it), so you can have a fair estimation of what to expect it to sell for.

I also advise you to research and have a look at the keywords other sellers of your item are using in their listing title. For example, if you were selling a 16GB iPod, you wouldn't just title your listing as "iPod 16GB". Rather, you would want to include as many relevant keywords as possible to describe your item and appeal to more searchers (keeping in mind you don't want to keyword stuff your title). A more appropriate title for an item like this would be, "Apple iPod 16GB MP3 Player 4th

Generation" – notice how this includes the brand name, a brief description of what the item is, and includes the model.

Obviously then, in your listing description, you would go into more detail about the item, including any aesthetic issues, as well as informing customers of the condition.

Again, I recommend looking at other sellers' listings of the same or similar items and taking notes. You can learn a lot about ways to lay out your listing description or keywords to include by researching what your competitors are doing (this applies when you are wanting to sell any type of item).

If you want more detailed advice about how to lay out your listing description and what to include, definitely check out my blog at The Big Venture. I regularly post tips on there about optimizing your eBay listings.

2) List for 10 days on a Thursday night

Once you've decided to list your item up as an auction, you may wonder how long you should list it for, and maybe when is the best time to list your item?

Firstly, the period of time of the highest traffic of potential buyers using eBay is in the evening, usually after the working hours, but most commonly on a Sunday night during around 4-9pm. Most people are winding down from the weekend and getting ready for the start of their week, and it can be assumed they're just doing some casual shopping on eBay and surfing the web.

If you're in the US, listing later in the evening EST time is most ideal since it will target both the east and west coasts of the country.

The point here, though, is not to bother listing your items in the morning or even the afternoon (and especially not in the middle of the night), since the "Best Match" function of the eBay search engine will display auctions ending soon, and targeting the right time will display your listing to the highest amount of people.

Also, by listing your auction for 10 days on a Thursday night, not only do you get longer exposure of your item to people, but you also get twice the exposure during the busy Sunday night (with the second exposure getting the most views and hopefully those big bids near the end of the auction!).

3) Start your auction at 99 cents

Despite what you may initially think, starting your auction at 99 cents is the best thing to do.

Why would I list an expensive item at 99 cents?

Remember that your initial auction price is merely a starting price, and there's a whole 10 days for your item to increase in price. The reason I advocate the 99 cents start price is because it will get the most amount of "Watchers" of your item, which could result in more bids near the ending days and hours of your auction.

For those who don't know, a watcher is a person who has basically put your item on their "My eBay" dashboard, allowing them to monitor the price for the duration of the listing. This is beneficial to us because they could start off as a watcher and become a bidder during the later stages of the auction.

If you price your item at a much higher price in an auction, odds are you will get a lot of people just skimming over it and not even bidding, let alone watching your item.

If you're worried about the price and think it may not sell for your expected price, you can always enter a "Reserve price". This means that the item will not sell if it ends on a bidding price of less than the "reserve price". It's basically an insurance of the sale price.

4) The more photos the better!

One of the most overlooked benefits when it comes to listing an item on eBay are photos!

Long story short, the more photos you add, the more your item will sell for.

eBay allows you to list up to 12 photos for free (the actual number depends on which country's eBay you're listing your item on), and unfortunately over 90% of eBay listings don't include more than 3 photos!

Think about it yourself, if you're looking to purchase a product, especially a product online, the more photos you can see of the item allows you to get a better understanding of what you'll be purchasing.

As a seller, it costs you nothing extra, simply snap several extra photos when you're about to list the item. Make sure you show all angles and aspects of the item you're selling too. And one final thing to note about lots of photos is it means less questions asked to you during the process of the listing!

Test, Test, Test

My advice here is based off everything I have learned in my years of selling items on eBay, as well as what has worked for me over the course of my selling career.

I always recommend people to test things out for themselves, and in the end, developing their own strategies, because for a certain item they may find something that works even better!

However, as a general starting point, especially if you're new to it and don't know much about selling items on eBay, I stick by my recommendations and I advise you to try what I suggest!

I've Sold Everything, Now What?

Okay, so now you have listed and sold all your unwanted (or unneeded) household items on eBay – what now?

Well, if you own the average amount of unwanted items the regular houschold has, you would have accrued a total of between $400 and $1,000 (hopefully the latter!). Remember that the items which will take you over the $500 line are going to be old cell phones, electronics, antiques, collector items (which you no longer want to hold onto) and brand-name clothing or shoes you don't really wear.

After all eBay fees, postage costs (which should have been included in the listing price), and PayPal fees, hopefully you have at least $500 in your PayPal account, which is going to be your starting capital. You can start with as little as $300, but for the best wholesale prices and diversification of products, the more the better.

With that said, you're now ready to take on Step 4 below…

Step 4 – Turning The $500 Into A Business

This is probably the most important step in this entire book because it determines how successful your eBay business will be. It is also the cornerstone of creating a solid stream of profit in your business.

Keep in mind that to begin with we're looking to simply sell products that will regularly sell at a profit. The big questions are of course, how do we determine what these products are? And where can we find these products?

Where can I get profitable products?

Your primary goal here is to be able to find products that you can purchase at a price below what you can sell it for. You need to also include all fees; therefore, the equation looks something like this:

Profit from your product sale =
Sale price of Product – (Original product cost + eBay fees + PayPal fees)

As you can see, the two parts of the equation we have control over are the sale price and original cost price. That being said, we do have limited control over the sale price, since we can maximize our marketing efforts, however it is still up to the demand to determine the price.

Therefore, it comes down to obtaining your products at the best possible cost price. Below I will discuss various places and ways to get cheap products that you can resell at a profit, and then further below I will share my advice on the best way to source a product or several products within the same niche so you can become a specialized seller.

A "niche", by the way, is essentially a category or topic. So, if you want to sell items in the playing cards niche, you would source various playing cards, in different brands, colors, sizes, shapes, etc., as long as you found they you could sell them for a profit! This is something I will also teach you below – so keep reading…

Keep in mind that we're starting off only using the capital we generated in the previous step, and our goal is to turn that money into more money, and eventually a system that will give us consistent profitable cash flow.

Garage Sales

I have to add this one in here because one of my good friends who runs their own eBay store, solely sources their products from two methods, one being garage sales (the other is finding "retail bargain" which I will explain in more detail below).

She makes anywhere from $2,000 to $6,000 a month depending on how much work she puts into going to multiple garage sales and finding bargains. Personally, it's not something I prefer because it requires more work than what I would actually want to do, but it is totally feasible.

The first step here is to find as many garages sales (or even cheap local markets) that are coming up in your area. I suggest doing a Google search for "garage sales in my area", "garage sale directory", "local garage sales", and so on. The reason is, depending on where you actually live, Google will display location-based results allowing you to find the most accurate results.

Doing a search like the one described above, I have already found nine separate websites which allow people to post the date and address of their upcoming garage sales, thereby promoting it.

Once you know where they are, you want to go check them out to find certain items that the owners don't know the real value of.

The best way to do this is by download the eBay app from the app store onto your cell phone and just casually searching up any items that strike your eye as potentially undervalued. You may be surprised with what you find!

There are times, however, you can just see an item, know its value based on your own experience, and confidently purchase it for the purpose of reselling.

I know some of you may be thinking, isn't that harsh on the original owners?

The truth is that many people running garage sales are either wanting quick cash or cleaning out old items from their house (if it's not the garage sale, it's the trash can). So, when you purchase items from them that you believe you can resell at a profit, it is a win-win situation.

When I first started selling items on eBay and had no real knowledge of wholesalers and suppliers, I did go to a few garage sales and resell some items – mainly undervalued books (this was before eBooks became so big!).

Please continue reading through the next few sections of this chapter because I will give you the biggest secret for an eBay seller to know if a product will sell for a profit or not!

Retail Bargains

You may look at "retail bargains" and think there is no way that you can find items online or in stores for below the price you can sell them on eBay!

While this, on the surface, is quite true. When you start digging deeper and looking for bargains, you will notice that there are many instances you can make anywhere from a 10% to 50% return on investment by selling an item you purchased straight from a retailer.

The first thing to do is find bargain websites or forums. The one I love the most for my personal use, but even to find some really good deals on items I can resell, is http://www.ozbargain.com.au.

I live in Australia, so it's specifically an Australian forum. You will notice by scrolling through it that the majority of deals on there that could be considered target items for an eBay reseller are from people finding bargains from online stores, loss leader marketing promotions by retailers (these are very common with new online retailers and can be

VERY profitable for an eBay seller), and even closing down sales.

If you can find bargain websites like the above in your local area (or that ship to your country if you're targeting online retailers), that's the best place to get started.

If you know any local stores closing down as well, go in and check out what they have for sale.

Just like with garage sales, I advise you to always be researching the items on eBay if you're unsure of how much they may go for.

As I mentioned before, please continue reading through the next few sections of this chapter because I will give you the biggest secret for an eBay seller to know if a product will sell for a profit or not!

Wholesalers

Okay so now we're going to discuss my favorite way to source products to resell, finding great wholesalers.

I'm going to break this down into three separate parts, and discuss them individually. I'll then go onto giving my recommendation about what I personally think is the most profitable and reliable.

1) Finding local wholesalers

Depending on where you live, and the fact that you're not running a massive enterprise, odds are you probably won't be able to start negotiating directly with suppliers just yet.

However, if you do some research and look up local wholesalers in your area (again, using my good friend Google!), you might actually find there are several depending on if you live in a big city or not.

In my city, Melbourne, Australia, there are many wholesalers that I can purchase products off, and the best part is that I only need a business tax number to be able to purchase from them.

When looking in your area, ideally the ones that are going to be the best to try out in the beginning are wholesalers that act somewhat like retailers but sell products in masses. Keep in mind if you require any business licenses to transact with wholesalers, do your research on that as well.

Also, one of the biggest limitations we have is that we are only working with a small amount of capital. A lot of wholesalers will have minimum quantities to purchase

2) Finding online wholesalers

Personally, I love to find and work with wholesalers and suppliers online. Why? Because it allows me to do business directly with companies all around the world. Also, because I'm sitting behind a computer in the comfort of my own home, I can thoroughly compare and calculate whether they offer me the best price of a product before I purchase from them.

So how do you find wholesalers?

It is actually fairly easy to find wholesalers and suppliers, only once you know the niche of the products you want to sell. So, have a read of this section now, but once I teach you below how to find popular trending eBay items and which niches are hot on eBay during certain seasons, which is in the steps below, come back and give this a read again!

Okay, so you have a rough idea of the niche or niches you want to create your store around, now we head over to Google once again and start digging through the massive Internet world for wholesalers we can work with that sell the products we are after.

Taking an example I used above, the playing cards niche, we can search things like "playing card wholesalers", "playing cards wholesale", "bulk playing cards", etc.

Doing this myself, what I've noticed is that there are many results including big name brand suppliers, such as Bicycle, and smaller wholesalers in my area, which presumably purchase larger lots from Bicycle and other brands of the same caliber.

At this point you need to filter out the big suppliers because you simply don't have the reach and capital to be sourcing products from them in the beginning. However, the smaller wholesalers definitely deserve looking into.

I also noticed that there are many listings of bulk playing cards sold in lots on eBay and Amazon.

This introduces into what I was going to discuss next: purchasing bulk lots from eBay and Amazon. I'm going to include this in the "online wholesalers" section because a lot of the sellers of these bulk lots are indeed wholesalers who are using eBay or Amazon as another medium to sell their item, albeit some are just regular people who might have sourced their own products from a wholesaler or supplier, and it went wrong.

Selling on eBay Australia, I had the advantage of purchasing many items from the US for a lower price. It's not a secret that many items sell in Australia for much more (sometimes two or three times as expensive) than they do in the US.

So, I would go through eBay and Amazon in search of people or wholesalers who could sell me bulk lots for a good price (including shipping of course). I'd then resell these on eBay Australia for a nice profit.

If you have the chance to do this (this doesn't just happen between the US and Australia, you can do this from your country and many others in the world, be it in Europe, the US, Australia, or even Asia – more on Asia below), definitely do your research into it and take advantage of it.

The way to find out if this is plausible for you is to extend your product research from Google to Amazon and country specific eBay websites. For example, to check out eBay UK, go to http://www.ebay.co.uk.

One last thing to mention is that I know from personal experience it's very easy to find wholesalers, but the part that is more difficult is of course finding *good* wholesalers.

To address this, I highly recommend <u>Salehoo</u>. It's a massive directory filled with over 8,000 filtered wholesalers. They are categorized for you as well, so you can go to your niche and see a nice list of potential wholesalers, hence saving you all that time you would have planned for research.

It does however cost you an annual fee to have access to the list. So, I only recommend it in the beginning if you have some extra money to spend. I personally found products myself for free and then once I started creating some profitable cash flow, I reinvested part of it into things like Salehoo to cut down my research time.

3) Online Wholesale Marketplaces

These websites are by far my favorite and the place I highly recommend you starting off when capital is low or when you are just beginning.

An online wholesale marketplace is effectively a place that allows factory owners, suppliers and wholesalers to connect with buyers (retailers, other wholesalers, individuals), somewhat like how eBay works. They are able to list their items and run online stores just like eBay would allow sellers to.

The best part about it is that you can chat live with the sellers directly and negotiate terms, quantities, or prices.

Keep in mind that the majority of online wholesale marketplaces are focused on giving sellers located in China a chance to sell to the rest of the world. This means that you will be dealing with a seller located in China, so you will need to learn about shipping methods from China to your home country (quite straight forward and presented on the websites themselves).

Below is a list of websites I recommend you to source your initial products from:

- http://www.dhgate.com
- http://www.alibaba.com
- http://www.aliexpress.com
- http://www.lightinthebox.com
- http://www.tomtop.com
- http://www.tradetang.com
- http://www.chinavasion.com
- http://www.made-in-china.com

7 Reasons Why Sourcing Products from China is the Best

Firstly, when I talk about sourcing products from China, I'm referring to the above websites, which contain wholesalers located in China. As stated already, I highly recommend looking into those websites to find your initial line of products, and these are the reasons I personally use them:

1) No minimum quantity (for the most part)

If you go onto one of the wholesale marketplace sites, for example DHGate, which is my personal favorite, and take a look at a few of the categories, you will notice the large number of sellers that sell the same products.

This is great for you, not only because you're going to get a better price (due to the competition), but because a lot of the sellers have no minimum quantity orders.

This means that you can purchase as little as 20 items of a particular product, or even one (more on that below).

The reason this is a positive for you is that it will allow you to enter markets and start finding profitable products without having to use all of our $500 initial capital!

2) Samples!

As mentioned briefly above, since there are no minimum quantity orders, you can find some sellers who will happily sell you one or two of a certain product.

This is a huge benefit for you because you can purchase a few items of several different products and test them out to see which one sells for the most!

Also, if you create a good relationship with any one particular wholesaler, you can negotiate free samples too!

3) Your payments are protected

I've already discussed how DHGate is by far my favorite, and another reason why I love using it so much is that all my payments made to wholesalers are fully protected by Escrow.

Escrow is a form of payment protection that basically means whenever I pay for products, my payment is held by a third party and is only cleared and deposited into the wholesaler's account once I have successfully received the items and there is nothing wrong with them.

I should also note that DHGate isn't the only site that utilizes an Escrow protection, many of the other wholesale marketplaces use some form of payment protection, and I highly recommend looking into that before using them.

4) High quality items or you can dispute

Most of the wholesale marketplace websites offer a dispute resolution function – I know DHGate does!

This is awesome for you because it means that the sellers are always forced to focus on both the quality of the products they are selling to you and the customer service they are providing.

If you receive any products that didn't match the description, weren't as described by the seller, or are just plain garbage, then you can dispute it with the seller and negotiate either a full or partial refund, or send the item back for a replacement. Remember the seller doesn't get the money in their account until you're happy!

5) Products come straight from suppliers or factories in China

Most of the products you purchase from sellers on these websites get the products straight from factories and suppliers directly in China that they work with.

This is a great thing for you because it means you can order customized versions of many products that are sold, or even get your own branding on them.

I have, many times, purchased customized clothing, wallets, belts, and sunglasses, which I negotiated directly with my wholesaler, who then got the items made especially for me by the factories.

6) You can get pretty much anything!

I know this is a huge claim, but if you actually utilize all the above wholesale marketplaces I stated, between all of them you can get nearly any item you would ever think of selling!

7) Build relationships that will benefit you in the long run

When you find really good wholesalers on any of the websites, usually the ones that have contact with various factories (so you can get access to numerous different product niches through the same wholesaler), I suggest building a long-term relationship with him or her.

If you can, talk to them about prices and even get them to price match other sellers (just so you keep building up the rapport between the both of you).

The reason this is beneficial is because eventually once you have both gotten to know each other and maybe done several transactions together, you can start working outside of the website.

Take DHGate for example. If I was to develop a great relationship with a particular seller, which I have done many times in the past, eventually they become my "go to" person whenever I want to test out a new product on eBay. I show them a picture, or give them the name, and they come back to me the next day with prices. Once it gets to this point, I personally like to work with them outside of DHGate, via email, Skype or over the phone.

Why? Because DHGate charges them fees! Yes, every time you purchase a lot of items off a seller through DHGate, the seller is charged a fee, and essentially it is YOU that pays. By taking the transaction and communication away from DHGate, whether through PayPal or another form, they don't have those DHGate fees to pay anymore and can reduce the prices for you!

Now, I need to point out here that this is technically against the DHGate policy. DHGate doesn't want sellers sharing their information to buyers, however if you purchase items from someone, they can send you contact details in the package or through a website link.

What I'm basically saying is that there are ways to work it out after a while once you begin to trust a certain seller or group of sellers, so that you can reduce overall purchasing costs. And aside from purchasing costs, it's just so much easier to be able to communicate through something like Skype than through DHGate messaging.

How to find profitable products

You're probably wondering at this point, "So Ashton, it's awesome to know where to find products, but how do I know which ones are profitable?"

Well, there are several ways you can find profitable products, and below I will go through several techniques to help you find profitable markets and products.

- *Using eBay popularity websites*

There are many websites around that will allow you to search through the most popular categories on eBay, or even the most searched keywords over a certain period of time.

Below is a small list of the ones I recommend:

- http://www.watchcount.com (will automatically identify your region)

- http://popular.ebay.com (change domain to .com.au for Australia, .co.uk for the UK, etc.)

- http://www.whatsellsbest.com/ (for USA only)

- http://popularproducts.co/ (for USA only)

When I first began I solely relied on WatchCount, which was enough for the research I required.

One important thing to note is to avoid any paid search tools because most of them are just filled with expensive data that isn't of any use to us small time eBay sellers (maybe something you look at later on).

- ***As Seen on TV & Infomercial Products***

This is exactly how I started off selling on eBay and where I made most of my initial profits.

As Seen on TV products (or any other major infomercial products) can be some of the most profitable products to sell on eBay, simply because the advertising has been done for you.

Whether you believe it or not, the majority of As Seen on TV products do sell quite well, either because they have been marketed incredibly well (most of them are!) or because they are actually pretty neat products.

However, a lot of the time these buyers may check on eBay before they call in, simply to see if it's cheaper – this is where you come into play!

The most awesome part here for you is that you can tap into that market by looking for the same or similar products and purchasing them straight from China from wholesalers who sell them.

Yes, it's really that simple and I recommend you starting here for the quickest and best results!

The first two products I sold on eBay were "Topsy Turvys" and "Slim N Lifts" – both As Seen on TV products, and they went wild. I was making between $50 to $150 *profit* a day selling these two products ($50 on slower days like Tuesdays and Wednesdays – up to $150+ on the weekends!).

Keep in mind that they were my first two products, so I was stoked to see my initial $500 grow well into four and even five figures over the course of a few months.

Now, there are three things you need to keep in mind about doing this.

1) You need to be on top of your research

If you're going to do this you must be ahead of the game and try to find products that are very new to the infomercial scene. These will be most profitable! Why? Keep reading…

2) As Seen on TV products can expire

Now, this doesn't apply to EVERY As Seen On TV Product, but it's the main reason why the majority of these products either get improved with time (new features, new bonuses, etc) or suddenly disappear off TV.

I personally can't say that I've seen an advertisement on TV for a Snuggie or Topsy Turvy recently – however, they *are* still being sold online (and maybe even in stores)!

Anyway, the point here is that if they eventually expire, your main goal is to get onto it as soon as you can, but also realize that you may have to one day move onto a new product. They aren't going to provide consistent and sustainable income in the long run unless you keep adapting to new trends and seasons depending on what consumers want.

3) Trademark laws, specifically VeRO

This point here is probably the most important thing you need to keep in mind.

All the products on TV are trademarked and some of the companies that sell them have rights on eBay that don't allow other sellers to use certain images, brand names, videos or even sell the product itself.

I highly suggest reading up more about this on eBay, but I will address this issue solely at the end of this chapter.

Anyway, back to teaching you how and where to find profitable products…

- *Use forums and blogs*

If you've already identified a niche (either in the beginning or further into your eBay selling career), I highly recommend looking up forums in that niche and just reading through some of the most common issues and problems that everyday people are facing.

Remember, these people are your buyers and if you can identify EXACTLY what issues they are having, you will get closer and closer to finding EXACTLY what products will consistently sell!

Take the card trick niche as an example (it was a niche I sold several products and ran my own eBay store in). When I first started selling things like card decks, invisible string, fake thumbs, and all sorts of other magic props, I simply looked at what sold well on eBay and also what I could source from my supplier at the time.

A couple of months later I began to play around with cards myself and even do a bit of street magic for fun, which led me to surfing magic and card trick forums for fun. Not only was I selling something which I thought was awesome, but I was also one of my own target market, and this taught me a lot more about the game of selling.

While surfing forums and reading blogs, I realized there were a few things that kept coming up over and over again, these "issues". One of which was about a magic prop that would regularly require replacement over and over again with use. I never even thought about selling it, but as soon as I did more research into it, and tried selling it, it became my biggest seller for that store!

My point here is that you can learn a lot about your own niche or items by simply putting yourself in the shoes of your target audience. Just like me, hopefully you can learn something you never knew before.

The Biggest Secret to Finding Profitable Products to Sell

As promised above, here is the biggest secret to finding profitable products to sell on eBay.

Using the above methods and resources, yes you can find plenty of fantastic products that can hopefully sell well on eBay, but without this secret right here, your entire eBay business could fall to pieces!

For some of you, this may not even be a secret, you may already know about this and use it extensively in your own product research, however, not only did it take me over 6 months to start using this tool effectively, but when working with my first 100 students and teaching them how to start their own eBay businesses, I found out that ONLY SIX of them knew about this before I told them!

So here it is…

- *The "Completed Listings" Feature on eBay*

What is "Completed Listings"?

It's a feature within the Advanced eBay Product Search that allows you to see all completed listings within a certain keyword search, both sold and unsold listings.

Therefore, it gives you access to the selling history of ANY PRODUCT you want!

If you still don't understand how this is so valuable, keep reading...

How is "Completed Listings" helpful to me?

Since it gives you full access to the selling history of any product you want to search for, you can determine the average prices it sells for!

Being able to determine a selling price for your item is probably one of the biggest advantages when it comes to product research!

Firstly, you'll be able to judge products before you even buy them (by comparing source prices to potential sale prices). Secondly, you can see if your item is a complete dud or the hottest thing on eBay right now (by comparing how many of the completed listings sold compared to how many didn't sell). Finally, you can spy on your competitors and see how they sell their items (listings, prices, selling formats, etc.)!

So, how do I use "Completed Listings"?

When you search for an item in eBay, right next to the search bar is a link titled "Advanced". Once you go into this, you will see a checkbox titled "Completed Listings" approximately in the middle of the page.

That's your money right there!

Test it out and try searching for any items you want, and tick the "Completed Listings" checkbox. Notice how the prices that are green refer to listings that were sold, and if they are red or black they didn't get sold/didn't get any bids.

You can also use this function on individual sellers and spy on your competitors!

I really do love the "Completed Listings" function and I hope you use it for everything it's worth because I honestly feel it's the most underrated tool on eBay and it can take you from being a hobby seller to doing this stuff as a full-time business!

VeRO – and what you can do about it

First, I need to point out that I'm simply providing information here and in no way am I competent at providing legal advice or provide any other professional services. If you require legal advice or expert assistance, the services of a competent professional should be sought.

Now that that's out of the way, here's what I do about working with VeRO restrictions.

I'm assuming that you already know what VeRO is, based on the brief description I wrote about above, if not, I highly recommend just typing "eBay VeRO" into Google and having a read about it straight from eBay themselves.

If you begin selling various items and stick to generic brands or non-branded items and use your own photographs and listings, there's a good chance you'll never run into any VeRO issues.

Mentioned on eBay is the list of reasons you can get pulled up on a VeRO infringement, and for the most part you should understand that you can sell plenty of items that are fine.

If you run into issues with VeRO a few times, it's as easy as just changing those products and finding new ones.

However, if you feel that you are at risk of a VeRO infringement or want to sell products that you feel might be a chance for an infringement, then this is what I recommend doing.

Create another eBay account – I have multiple accounts, it's not against policy, each account usually sells a specific niche of products, and then I have another account just for buying items. On this new account (or on your buying account) simply list up the item you are planning to buy from China *BEFORE* you buy it and see if it gets taken down.

Now, the first thing you have to do is in the listing specify that it's a "pre-order" of the item and it will only be available on a specified date, or price it at a higher than market value so it probably won't sell just yet anyway.

Doing this before you have purchased the item in a mass amount from China means that you don't have to risk any money in case the item does turn out to be VeRO restricted, and this is a huge positive for you.

I also noted to do it on another account because we don't want to risk any infringements on our first priority selling account (eBay will rate your account based on your compliance with their policies). While good selling will always outweigh any infringements in time, it's wise not to infringe if you can help it.

Now that I know everything, how do I put it all together?

In this step, I've given you a lot of different ideas, plans and resources that you now need to put together. Here's how:

The first step is to research and find one or more products to sell that can either be in the same niche or different niches to begin with.

This is where I recommend firstly going through sites like WatchCount to generate some idea of what categories are hot or the type of product lines that can generate a lot of sales.

Once you have identified a niche, you can research it more by reading through forums, or even just looking through the related categories on eBay or sites like DHGate to see what products you could potentially buy and resell.

Finally, don't forget to use the "Completed Listings" search to ensure you can actually sell products for a profit before you even import them!

I've written a detailed instructional guide showing exactly how I go through all of the steps myself, and I discuss little strategies that help me. You can get it here absolutely FREE!

http://www.thebigventure.com/ebay-business-action-plan/

Now that you have what you need to begin creating some product lines in your eBay store, it's time to take a look at other very important aspects that will allow you to be successful.

Step 5 – Treating It Like a Business

At this point you should be quite aware of how to source products, effectively test new product lines and eventually roll out profitable products into the market.

What matters now is how you treat your business, and more importantly, how you treat your customers.

Stay Professional

Despite you and your customers completing these transactions behind a computer screen, remember that there are real people on the other side.

This is where you can tell the difference between an eBay store that's just a hobby that someone does in their spare time, and one that's a full-time store run professionally, because it all comes how you treat your customers.

The best tip I can give you here is to just remember that they are real people. Check your eBay messages regularly (I always used to hook it up to my smart phone so I could get an alert whenever someone messaged me on eBay), because when you reply fast to questions or queries, customers love it.

Also, keep your listings very professional and to the point. The more information you include, the less likely you are to face questions from customers.

Return Policy

It's completely up to you whether or not you want to offer returns on your items, however, I recommend offering "returns on unopened items for up to 30 days".

This will allow you to benefit from the increased sales that you wouldn't normally receive if you just wrote "NO REFUNDS ACCEPTED", and the truth is that not many people refund anyways.

If someone does decide to ask for a refund, since it's on unopened items, providing it's not faulty, you can just relist it and sell it again.

Warranty

Again, it's completely up to you if you want to offer a warranty or not, but it puts customers' minds at ease when deciding to make a sale, especially electronics.

I recommend offering a warranty of 12-months because it will keep your customers at peace, and it also benefits you because it's effectively a two-month warranty for you. The reason is because after the first two months the number of warranty claims is effectively zero.

Even in the first two months, you will barely face any issues with warranties unless you're selling a poor-quality product (which hopefully you have checked or tested out first).

Shipping

If you can, offer multiple shipping methods depending on the speed of delivery.

Personally, I like to offer free shipping as the base line for standard delivery, and then have two extra options, one for express shipping and another for express *and* insured shipping.

From what I have tested, customers are more likely to purchase your items if they are given a free shipping option, and if they require it faster they will voluntarily make use of your other options.

Handling Customer Questions

The most important thing to do when answering customer questions to reply back as soon as you can since this could be the deciding factor for some customers and purchasing your product.

How?

Because it's common for buyers to find a few sellers of a product (usually with similar prices) and ask a question about features, which turns out to be the deciding factor.

Personally, I do this myself, especially if I find a similar product and need to know something about it, I'll message a few sellers and the first person to tell me that the product has what I need is the person I will buy it from.

The second thing to keep in mind with customer questions is that if you are getting too many, you're doing something wrong. You need to prevent being asked questions as much as you can, and the best way to do this is to include a FAQ section in your listings at the bottom.

It will be a generic one with information on shipping, returns, warranties, etc., and it will serve to answer the generic questions that don't pertain to your specific items but will prevent basic recurring questions.

Feedback Rating

Your feedback rating is very important and you should strive to keep it at 100%.

Here are some great tips to keep your feedback rating as high as possible:

1) *Never lie in your listings – tell your customers what to expect and when they get it they will be happy.*

2) *If you're selling a used item and there are aesthetic issues, always take clear photos of these issues and detail them appropriately.*

3) *Ship your items out as soon as possible after you are paid for them.*

4) *If you receive and questions or messages regarding the transaction or item, aim to reply back as soon as possible and be of help!*

5) *Pack your items well when you ship them so they don't get damaged in transit.*

6) *Price your shipping prices at fair prices. If it's not free shipping then ensure it's a realistic price so you can get higher feedback ratings.*

7) *Don't sell faulty or problematic items!*

8) *Give refunds when necessary because sometimes the cost of a refund could spare your reputation.*

If you find yourself receiving an unfair negative feedback rating then you can actually reply back to it and state your view on it for future buyers to see. In some cases, you can message the buyer directly and try to sort out a way to get it revised.

Detailed Seller Ratings

In addition to your feedback rating you also get "Detailed Seller Ratings" which outline how you perform on the following four factors:

- Item as described
- Communication
- Shipping time
- Shipping and handling charges

These factors get rated on a 5-star scale, and if you use the free shipping option you automatically get 5 stars for shipping and handling charges (highly recommended!).

If you include detailed listings, reply to messages as soon as possible, and ship your items out as soon as possible, you should expect good ratings for these factors as well.

Step 6 – Tips to SMASH the Competition

Right now, you have what you need to get started selling on eBay and learn as you go, building on the knowledge you have learned thus far.

That being said, here are some of my favorite tips that I believe will take you from being an average eBay seller to one of the top few!

Remember not to just read it, but actually implement these when you can!

Note: I may repeat a few things from the above chapters, but it's only for your benefit because I feel that they are important things to know.

1) Always use the "Completed Listings" function to research your products before you decide to invest in it. This is covered in more detail in "Step 4" of this book.

2) Starting auctions at 99 cents attracts the most people in the beginning (as watchers) and can increase the amount of bidding of your item, especially near the end of the auction.

3) Auction duration isn't a big deal as long as the auction is ending on a Sunday night since that is considered one of the busiest times on eBay (so your auction will appear higher on the "Best Match" searches of your item). Shorter auctions are great for products you want to sell quickly or

have a lot of so you can speed up turnover. If you have something rare that has lower demand, go for 7 or 10 days!

4) If you have multiple products of an identical item and you item sells as an auction for a high price, look to offer "Second Chance Offers" to the losing bidders who have bid satisfactory prices. For example, you're selling Product A and you want $100 for it. It sells for $185 with three other bidders who have bid at least $100 each. You can offer a "Second Chance Offer" to the other three bidders for their maximum bid price and hopefully sell more of your items quicker (no listing fees too!).

5) Use urgency keywords in your listing such as "Limited Stock", "For a limited time only" and "End of season sale". These will cause a sense of urgency in the buyer and may lead to more sales (especially buy-it-now items).

6) Ensure your listing title has the keywords that will be searched for your product. For example, if you're selling an Apple iPhone 3GS, include those keywords, "apple", "iphone", "3gs", and also consider including things like your store ("16gb"), as well as whether it's "brand new" or "used", and also if it's "unlocked" or branded by a provider.

7) Inside your listing descriptions try to focus on benefits of a product rather than features. This is

a very powerful and general marketing technique that can be used to sell anything because it makes features relatable to the customer. For example, if I was selling a mobile Internet service to a potential buyer, instead of saying "LTE Internet speeds", which could be absolute gibberish to some customers, I would say "Never wait for your YouTube videos or music to buffer ever again!" Notice how it's more relatable to issues that the everyday person would face, and how my "feature" actually solves a problem and becomes a "benefit".

8) Include at least one smiley face in your product listing! It makes the listing friendlier and despite thinking it may look unprofessional, it actually gives the listing a personal touch. If you're afraid, try to split test it and have two identical auctions, one with the smiley faces, and one without, and see which sells for a better price!

9) As already mentioned, free shipping is the best thing you can offer. It is proven to increase sales and can also increase feedback ratings.

10) Don't fall for all the extra bells and whistles on your listings, like "bold titles" and "subtitles". Unless they are free (for a promotion), they are a waste of money and I don't recommend using them!

11) Use as many photos as you can in your listing because the more photos you have the more your

item will go for (in an auction). For a buy-it-now listing it will seller quicker with more photos. This is because customers are very visual and want to see their product. Even include an embedded YouTube video in the description if you know how to (Google "embed YouTube video in eBay listing").

12)   Create your listing description and use different fonts, font sizes and/or colors. This will make your listing stand out, easier to read, and allow you to include more information without it seeming cluttered.

13)   For the rest of my eBay selling tips, check out my blog at <u>The Big Venture</u>. I regularly blog about new tips and tricks I discover and you can read about them there!

Step 7 – Making Six Figures on eBay

This is the final step in the process of creating a successful eBay business and it's basically the essential step that will allow you to take your business from something small to something life changing!

Hopefully when you have started selling on eBay (if you haven't already), and you get to this point in your eBay business career, you have a set amount of processes already in order and it's a matter of just doing it (and being creative of course!).

This is where automation comes into play and it's the stairs that will lead you to the big bucks! Without automation, you will either be slaving away for many, many hours each and every day on your eBay business, whether that be to research items, list them, or ship them, or you will suddenly find that your income is plateauing and you have no idea why.

Automation is going to give you more time to work ON your business rather than IN your business. This is crucial if you want to take your business further. Below are strategies that you can apply to begin automation and then take your skills to the next level.

Automation Tools

Turbo Lister

This is a tool I highly recommend for small and medium sized eBay businesses because it will allow you to start automating some of the more basic things such as listings.

Best of all it's a tool that can be downloaded directly from eBay for free (just Google it).

Turbo Lister simply lets you work on your listings offline, plugging all your listings into the software while you're offline, bit by bit or all at once, and then uploading them together at your discretion when you are online.

Why is it beneficial to me?

It's fantastic because it means you won't be losing any of your listings while you're creating them online (you won't believe how many times I've accidently clicked "Refresh" or "Back" in my browser while I am creating a listing).

Also, it allows you to create all your listings in one go, at any time in the week, and upload them at a more appropriate time (to maximize auction sales!).

Selling Manager

Selling Manager is a tool that you can use to help you sell your items on eBay. It's available online and doesn't require any downloads.

You can Google it and find it (it's affiliated with eBay), and it's free! It is, however, a more limited version of Selling Manager Pro, which requires a paid subscription.

Using this tool, you can have all your product listings and item information in one place, never missing a thing!

Also, it groups all your items together so you can more easily complete bulk tasks, such as listing items, relisting items, leaving feedback, sending messages, invoicing and printing shipping labels.

Why is it beneficial to me?

Using Selling Manager, you can speed up the amount of time you spend on basic tasks required to sell items, invoice customers, print shipping labels and leave feedback.

This will give you more time to do other important things like physically ship the items, or even search for new product lines.

Selling Manager Pro

Selling Manager Pro is pretty much the same as Selling Manager, except it has a few added benefits.

It's also a paid program that requires you to subscribe. It costs approximately $10 a month; however, the actual price depends on your location and which country's eBay you intend to use it on.

Why is it beneficial to me?

This is where the true benefits of automation come into play.

Firstly, using the Pro version will allow you to print out detailed sales records and evaluations which can help you to see which products are selling better than others, and at what times and days (so you can maximize auction sales!).

Also, you can monitor accurate inventory details, like keeping count of how much stock you have left without checking in your garage or shed.

This is my favorite benefit of using Selling Manager Pro – you can automatic those mundane tasks such as emailing customers after they purchase items, pay for items, or items are marked as shipped. You can automate feedback, and even automate relisting schedules and relisting of unsold items.

Like I said above, this is where the true benefits of automation come into play because you suddenly start to see massive decreases in the amount of time you spend online, and when you are online, you're just managing your business because everything, especially the mundane tasks, are automatically done for you.

Shipworks

This is a tool that is awesome for US eBay sellers (unfortunately due to the specific programming required for each shipping provider it's only available in the US as of time of writing this eBook).

It's a tool that will automatically take the shipping addresses of your completed listings and imports the recipient information into your shipping carrier's online shipping forms. It's linked to many US carriers, such as Fedex and UPS, plus a few more!

Why is it beneficial to me?

This will save you so much time writing out or even printing shipping labels, making things much easier when it comes to the shipping part of your business.

Other automated listing software

Here are some more programs and online tools you can use. I haven't discussed them individually because I only really have ever used both Turbo Lister and Selling Manager Pro myself. I have messed around with Auctiva before, but not for too long.

Here's the list:

- http://www.auctiva.com
- http://www.auctionwizard.com
- http://www.marketblast.com
- http://www.vendio.com

Automation: in a whole new light!

This idea I'm about to write about might seem quite ridiculous on how much your business is making, but it's something you need to consider when you start getting bigger (which may only be once you move to your own website – more on this below!).

I'm talking about hiring someone to work in your business for you.

Personally, I hired some young students to help me out with the shipping side of things because I just didn't have the time, nor did I want to print out shipping labels, pack items, and go to the post office every day.

Combining this with the automation tools I used for listing new products, I had most of my business automated, and found that the only time I spent online was to work on researching new products and markets. This allowed me to spend more time working on my business rather than in my business, and it's the secret to how I could grow things much quicker!

If that's something you can't do, maybe consider someone in your family? A brother? Sister? Mother? Grandparent?

Is there anyone around you that can help you out for an hour or so a day with your business?

When hiring someone "in real life", it's usually for your physical work, such as shipping.

The reason I say, "in real life" is because you can actually hire a virtual assistant to help you out with the virtual work, such as listings, feedback, etc., especially if you don't want to invest in an automation tool.

I recommend checking out http://www.elance.com or http://www.odesk.com to find people you can hire.

Simply post up a job with the work you're offering, such as "eBay listing creation" and test out a few workers with some small jobs.

I do this myself and once I find someone that can perform the tasks I need at a reasonable level, I usually hire them for a month to test them out. If there are no issues, I keep them longer!

Definitely check out both those sites, and even read up on some tutorials on how they work so you can learn more about it. Unfortunately, I can't go into much detail about it here because I can ramble on about it so much that it would fit into another eBook of its own. However, you can read up about it on my blog!

Creating an eBay Store

If you haven't already, consider opening up an eBay store instead of just selling your items regularly.

An eBay store has a monthly cost; however, you do get cheaper listing fees and a few other discounts like that, which will make it a beneficial investment once you begin selling higher volumes of products.

Also, it gives you a more professional feel and look online, which can help increase sales.

Where the real growth of your online business comes is below...

Creating your own eCommerce website

Once you have proved to yourself that you have found several products that are creating a lot of profit for yourself, it's time to increase your profit by removing eBay fees out of the equation.

You can do this by moving out on your own and creating your very own eCommerce website.

There are many ways you can do this, but it comes down to buying a domain, getting some web hosting, and then implementing a shopping cart on your site that allows you to accept payments online.

Again, I can ramble for hours about this and unfortunately, I can't include any more than a few lines about this, but it's an idea I am presenting you.

I actually have another eBook currently in creation stage about this whole transition from eBay to your own website, so keep checking my blog for the release date!

That being said, if you already know how to create your own website, the transition from eBay to your own site comes down to a movement of reputation and customers.

This can be done through several methods but the most effective are below:

- Have some sort of connection from your eBay listings to your website, whether it be a graphic or a link (if you can get away with it on eBay). Emphasize a discounted price if you can!

- Include business cards to your website in all your packages, and offer future sale discounts via coupons!

- Utilize bargain websites such as http://www.ozbargain.com.au and try to generate buzz and a customer base in the beginning through strong loss leader marketing campaigns.

Using these techniques, you can start to see a transfer of reputation and customer base from your eBay store to your website, and that's how you can fast track your website growth!

Conclusion

At the end of the day, no matter what you have learned through reading my eBook, it all comes down to the action you take.

You won't get any results just reading this eBook and then never thinking about it again.

You won't even get any results reading this eBook and then listing up one or two items.

If you really want eBay success, you need to implement everything I am teaching you and doing it properly, with persistence!

Running an eBay business is not a get-rich-quick scheme, it's something that you need to build from scratch and nourish with determination. Only then will you begin to see the long-lasting results.

Finally, just remember it's possible and once you get the ball rolling you'll see it's actually not as hard as it might seem!

Final Words

I would like to thank you again for downloading this book and hope that I have been able to help or even guide you on your journey to creating a successful eBay business of your own!

If you have enjoyed this book and would like to share your positive thoughts, could you please take 30 seconds of your time to go back and give me a review on my Amazon book page!

I greatly appreciate seeing these reviews because it helps me share my hard work!

Again, thank you and I wish you all the best with your eBay endeavors!

PS: Don't forget you can contact me via my blog at http://www.thebigventure.com

Disclaimer

I have created this eBook with the purpose to provide information on eBay selling and running an eCommerce business.

It is sold with the understanding that the author and publisher are not engaged in any sort of professional services or legal advice.

Every effort has been made to ensure this book is complete and without error, however it's possible that there may be errors, whether in content or other.

Therefore, do not consider this to be anything more than a guide and a book created for entertainment purposes.

The author and publisher are not liable or responsible for any damages or losses incurred by any person, which has been allegedly been caused directly or indirectly by the information within this book.

If you do not agree with the above information, simply contact the author for a full refund.